The Essentia

LAND

DISCOVERY

Series 1 1989 to 1998

Your marque expert:
James Taylor

 MW00528048

VELOCE PUBLISHING
THE PUBLISHER OF FINE AUTOMOTIVE BOOKS

Essential Buyer's Guide Series

Alfa Romeo Alfasud (Metcalfe)
Alfa Romeo Alfetta: all saloon/sedan models 1972 to 1984 & coupé models 1974 to 1987 (Metcalfe)
Alfa Romeo Giulia GT Coupé (Booker)
Alfa Romeo Giulia Spider (Booker)
Audi TT (Davies)
Audi TT Mk2 2006 to 2014 (Durnan)
Austin-Healey Big Healeys (Trummel)
BMW Boxer Twins (Henshaw)
BMW E30 3 Series 1981 to 1994 (Hosier)
BMW GS (Henshaw)
BMW X5 (Saunders)
BMW Z3 Roadster (Fishwick)
BMW Z4: E85 Roadster and E86 Coupe including M and Alpina 2003 to 2009 (Smitheram)
BSA 350, 441 & 500 Singles (Henshaw)
BSA 500 & 650 Twins (Henshaw)
BSA Bantam (Henshaw)
Choosing, Using & Maintaining Your Electric Bicycle (Henshaw)
Citroën 2CV (Paxton)
Citroën ID & DS (Heilig)
Cobra Replicas (Ayre)
Corvette C2 Sting Ray 1963-1967 (Falconer)
Datsun 240Z 1969 to 1973 (Newlyn)
DeLorean DMC-12 1981 to 1983 (Williams)
Ducati Bevel Twins (Falloon)
Ducati Desmodue Twins (Falloon)
Ducati Desmoquattro Twins – 851, 888, 916, 996, 998, ST4 1988 to 2004 (Falloon)
Fiat 500 & 600 (Bobbitt)
Ford Capri (Paxton)
Ford Escort Mk1 & Mk2 (Williamson)
Ford Model A – All Models 1927 to 1931 (Buckley)
Ford Model T – All Models 1909 to 1927 (Barker)
Ford Mustang – First Generation 1964 to 1973 (Cook)
Ford Mustang (Cook)
Ford RS Cosworth Sierra & Escort (Williamson)
Harley-Davidson Big Twins (Henshaw)
Hillman Imp (Morgan)
Hinckley Triumph triples & fours 750, 900, 955, 1000, 1050, 1200 – 1991-2009 (Henshaw)
Honda CBR FireBlade (Henshaw)
Honda CBR600 Hurricane (Henshaw)
Honda SOHC Fours 1969-1984 (Henshaw)
Jaguar E-Type 3.8 & 4.2 litre (Crespin)
Jaguar E-type V12 5.3 litre (Crespin)
Jaguar Mark 1 & 2 (All models including Daimler 2.5-litre V8) 1955 to 1969 (Thorley)
Jaguar New XK 2005-2014 (Thorley)
Jaguar S-Type – 1999 to 2007 (Thorley)
Jaguar X-Type – 2001 to 2009 (Thorley)
Jaguar XJ-S (Crespin)
Jaguar XJ6, XJ8 & XJR (Thorley)
Jaguar XK 120, 140 & 150 (Thorley)
Jaguar XK8 & XKR (1996-2005) (Thorley)
Jaguar/Daimler XJ 1994-2003 (Crespin)
Jaguar/Daimler XJ40 (Crespin)
Jaguar/Daimler XJ6, XJ12 & Sovereign (Crespin)
Kawasaki Z1 & Z900 (Orritt)
Land Rover Discovery Series 1 (1989-1998) (Taylor)
Land Rover Discovery Series 2 (1998-2004) (Taylor)
Land Rover Series I, II & IIA (Thurman)
Land Rover Series III (Thurman)
Lotus Seven replicas & Caterham 7: 1973-2013 (Hawkins)
Mazda MX-5 Miata (Mk1 1989-97 & Mk2 98-2001) (Crook)
Mazda RX-8 (Parish)
Mercedes Benz Pagoda 230SL, 250SL & 280SL roadsters & coupés (Bass)
Mercedes-Benz 190: all 190 models (W201 series) 1982 to 1993 (Parish)
Mercedes-Benz 280-560SL & SLC (Bass)
Mercedes-Benz SL R129-series 1989 to 2001 (Parish)
Mercedes-Benz SLK (Bass)
Mercedes-Benz W123 (Parish)
Mercedes-Benz W124 – All models 1984-1997 (Zoporowski)
MG Midget & A-H Sprite (Horler)
MG TD, TF & TF1500 (Jones)
MGA 1955-1962 (Crosier)
MGB & MGB GT (Williams)
MGF & MG TF (Hawkins)
Mini (Paxton)
Morris Minor & 1000 (Newell)
Moto Guzzi 2-valve big twins (Falloon)
New Mini (Collins)
Norton Commando (Henshaw)
Peugeot 205 GTI (Blackburn)
Piaggio Scooters – all modern two-stroke & four-stroke automatic models 1991 to 2016 (Willis)
Porsche 911 (964) (Streather)
Porsche 911 (993) (Streather)
Porsche 911 (996) (Streather)
Porsche 911 (997) – Model years 2004 to 2009 (Streather)
Porsche 911 (997) – Second generation models 2009 to 2012 (Streather)
Porsche 911 Carrera 3.2 (Streather)
Porsche 911SC (Streather)
Porsche 924 – All models 1976 to 1988 (Hodgkins)
Porsche 928 (Hemmings)
Porsche 930 Turbo & 911 (930) Turbo (Streather)
Porsche 944 (Higgins)
Porsche 981 Boxster & Cayman (Streather)
Porsche 986 Boxster (Streather)
Porsche 987 Boxster and Cayman 1st generation (2005-2009) (Streather)
Porsche 987 Boxster and Cayman 2nd generation (2009-2012) (Streather)
Range Rover – First Generation models 1970 to 1996 (Taylor)
Rolls-Royce Silver Shadow & Bentley T-Series (Bobbitt)
Royal Enfield Bullet (Henshaw)
Subaru Impreza (Hobbs)
Sunbeam Alpine (Barker)
Triumph 350 & 500 Twins (Henshaw)
Triumph Bonneville (Henshaw)
Triumph Stag (Mort)
Triumph Thunderbird, Trophy & Tiger (Henshaw)
Triumph TR6 (Williams)
Triumph TR7 & TR8 (Williams)
Velocette 350 & 500 Singles 1946 to 1970 (Henshaw)
Vespa Scooters – Classic 2-stroke models 1960-2008 (Paxton)
Volkswagen Bus (Copping)
Volvo 700/900 Series (Beavis)
Volvo P1800/1800S, E & ES 1961 to 1973 (Murray)
VW Beetle (Copping)
VW Golf GTI (Copping)

www.veloce.co.uk

First published in June 2018 by Veloce Publishing Limited, Veloce House, Parkway Farm Business Park, Middle Farm Way, Poundbury, Dorchester DT1 3AR, England. Tel +44 (0)1305 260068 / Fax 01305 250479 / e-mail info@veloce.co.uk / web www.veloce.co.uk or www.velocebooks.com. ISBN: 978-1-787112-41-4 UPC: 6-36847-01241-0.

Introduction
– the purpose of this book

This book will help you buy a first-generation Discovery that suits your needs and budget. Generally speaking, enthusiasts and those in the trade will call all 1989-1998 Discoverys 'Discovery 1' types, but they actually fall into two sub-types. There are the early ones, introduced in late 1989 for the 1990 model-year, and the 'face-lifted' versions, which arrived in March 1994 for the 1995 model-year. The last Discovery 1 was built in mid-1998, before it was replaced by the similar-looking, but more sophisticated, Discovery Series II.

The Discovery 1 was introduced to give Land Rover a strong-selling model in the emerging market for family-oriented 4x4s. The company's Range Rover model had, to a large extent, established passenger-carrying 4x4s in Europe (although there had been precedents in the USA), but it had become too expensive to sell in large numbers. There had also been several much less expensive imitations during the 1980s, especially from Japanese makers, and these had been deliberately designed as 'more adventurous' alternatives to a conventional family estate car. The Discovery was drawn up to claim as much of that market as possible for Land Rover.

To minimise development costs and get the Discovery into production as quickly as possible, Land Rover based it on the Range Rover's chassis. To reduce costs further and differentiate between the two models, the Discovery did without

Fondly remembered – for its thirst, at least.

the Range Rover's self-levelling rear suspension. A very different body did the rest. The Discovery was given a stepped roofline to allow headroom for two extra passengers in the rear. The first ones produced were all three-door types (two side doors and one tail door), and were joined a year later by five-door types (four side doors and one tail door). Seating was for five or, at an extra cost, seven, when two inward-facing 'occasional' seats were fitted in the load area.

Although the Range Rover's V8 petrol engine did appear in the Discovery with a lower state of tune, it was only used in about 20% of those sold. By far, the majority of Discoverys had a much more frugal four-cylinder diesel engine called the Tdi, meaning it was turbocharged and had a direct-injection fuel system. The first models had the 200Tdi, and a considerably more refined (but no more powerful) 300Tdi version was introduced with the face-lift in 1994. As the Tdi engine was central to the Discovery range, the early models are sometimes called the '200 series,' and the later ones the '300 series,' regardless of whether a diesel engine was fitted or not.

There was also a four-cylinder Rover petrol/gasoline engine, between 1992 and 1997, called the Mpi, which was below two litres in capacity, to suit tax regulations in some countries. It was never very popular in the UK.

The Discovery became Land Rover's best-selling model, and from 1994 it swelled the company's model range in the USA as well. Land Rover built 392,443 vehicles altogether, which means there's no shortage of examples to choose from. Although many have been modified or turned into off-road specials (and many more have decayed beyond hope when repairs became too expensive for their owners), thankfully, there are still many good ones left to enjoy.

Thanks

I was lucky enough to be invited to all the major ride-and-drive events for UK media after the Discovery's introduction in 1989, and I've driven more examples than I care to remember. Thanks, then, must go to Land Rover for providing those opportunities; and thanks, too, to Stan Tooth at Turbo 4x4 in Reading, who looked after a rather nice (if terribly thirsty) 1996 V8i model with the top ES trim on behalf of the Taylor family. That Discovery is now gone, but is definitely not forgotten.

Contents

The Essential Buyer's Guide™ currency
At the time of publication a BG unit of currency "●" equals approximately
£1.00/US$1.42/Euro 1.14. Please adjust to suit current exchange rates.

1 Is it the right car for you?
– marriage guidance

Tall and short drivers

Tall drivers are easily accommodated; there's plenty of legroom and decent overhead space in the front seat. Good seat adjustment means that short drivers will be just as happy in a Discovery too.

Pre-1995, the heating and ventilation controls were less than straightforward.

The controls on later models were a vast improvement on the originals.

Controls

Important switches are on the instrument binnacle, easily accessible. Heating, ventilation, and air-con controls are a mishmash on pre-1995 models; learn them before driving. Manual gearboxes aren't slick, although the later R380 is better than the early LT77. Smaller drivers sometimes complain of a heavy clutch.

Will it fit in the garage?

A first-generation Discovery is 178in (4521mm) long, 70.6in (1793mm) wide over its door mirrors, and 77.5in (1968mm) tall with roof bars, 75.6in (1930mm) without. This means it won't fit into some domestic garages, so check yours! You may also have to fold the door mirrors to get through a standard garage door.

Interior space

Discoverys come as five-seaters or seven-seaters. The two extra seats are inward-facing folding seats placed in the load area; when fitted they occupy space otherwise given to storage bins. Legroom in these seats is limited, and they're best suited to children. You can seat three on the rear (middle) bench, but legroom behind a tall driver may be restricted.

Too close for comfort: with roof bars, this Discovery is a very tight fit under a standard up-and-over garage door.

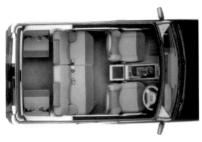

Split-folding rear seats on all models make the most of the loadspace in the rear. This is a seven-seater.

Even with the rear seat in place (the backrest is folded here), the load area is still spacious, as demonstrated here.

Luggage capacity
The load area will easily hold normal amounts of holiday luggage for four people or, if stacked a little higher, for five. However, loadspace is negligible if the folding seats are in use. The split-folding rear (middle) bench makes the loadspace versatile.

Usability
Acceleration of the diesel models is leisurely, but cruising speeds wholly acceptable. The brakes are excellent. Running costs of diesel engines are reasonable; petrol engines less so.

The early interior is much more spartan than the later one; often in bright Sonar Blue, as here.

Parts availability
Keep a Discovery running by using consumable parts from specialists. The supply of body panels and structural parts is gradually dwindling, although some items have been remanufactured by aftermarket suppliers.

Plus points
This is an excellent towing vehicle with formidable off-road ability. It's generally rugged and long-lasting, and most essential maintenance can be done on a DIY basis.

The 1995 and later models have a completely different dashboard, and different upholstery, too. All UK (and US) examples had twin-airbag installations as well.

Minus points
The build quality of all Discoverys was sometimes questionable, and the V8 petrol models are thirsty and costly to run.

2 Cost considerations
– affordable, or a money pit?

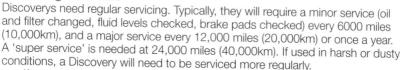

Servicing intervals

Discoverys need regular servicing. Typically, they will require a minor service (oil and filter changed, fluid levels checked, brake pads checked) every 6000 miles (10,000km), and a major service every 12,000 miles (20,000km) or once a year. A 'super service' is needed at 24,000 miles (40,000km). If used in harsh or dusty conditions, a Discovery will need to be serviced more regularly.

If you go to a specialist, the minor service will cost around ●x150, and the major service around ●x200, plus the cost of any additional parts, such as new brake pads, spark plugs, etc. The super service will be around ●x400. Land Rover franchised dealers will be more expensive than independent specialists.

Sample parts prices

Please note: prices can vary considerably, and the cheapest isn't always the best option, nor is the most expensive! Many pattern parts are available, but not all are made to OE standards; the prices shown are typical, but you will find a wide variation. All prices are before VAT is added.

Alternator: 100amp type	●x115	V8, stainless steel		●x325
Brake pads: front axle set	●x20	**Radiator:**		
Rear axle set	●x15	V8 manual, aftermarket		●x165
Bumper: front, bar only	●x103	V8 automatic, aftermarket		●x153
Rear, aftermarket	●x130	Tdi, aftermarket		●x63
Exhaust system: 200Tdi,		**Shock absorber:** aftermarket		
aftermarket	●x60	performance type		●x55
200Tdi, stainless steel	●x325	**Steering damper**		●x15
300Tdi, aftermarket	●x81	**Tyres** (depending on type)		●x60
V8, no catalyst, aftermarket	●x144	**Wiper blade**		●x4
V8, catalyst, aftermarket	●x285			

Parts that are easy to find

Most mechanical items and consumables are readily available, but in some cases you may have to compromise on quality. Some inner-body items (sills, rear crossmember, boot floor) have been remanufactured.

Parts that are hard to find

Body side decals for early models are hard to come by.

Beware!

Some Discoverys have been re-engined with non-Land Rover engines, typically diesels. There's nothing intrinsically wrong with this (unless you are a stickler for originality), but do make sure that you are able to find spares for the non-original engine. Most ordinary Land Rover specialists are unlikely to stock them.

3 Living with a Discovery
– will you get along together?

Much of the pleasure of Discovery ownership comes from knowing the vehicle will get you where you're going, whatever the weather. That's not to say that Discoverys have faultless reliability, but their four-wheel drive gives them excellent traction and roadholding in wet conditions, and the ability to press on through snow if necessary. A bonus is that you can see over most other traffic to anticipate problems ahead. Whether driving on a motorway, in traffic, or in low ratio off-road, a Discovery feels safe and dependable.

From the start, the Discovery was deliberately designed to be a practical family vehicle; there's room for fairly large loads in the back, and the split-fold rear seats give versatility for longer loads. The seven-seater option allows for more passengers too. There are lots of small stowage spaces (above the sun visors, in door pockets, in roof nets at the rear, in the centre cubby box), although these are rather less practical than they appear at first sight. Many people bought, and still buy, Discoverys because they're excellent for towing caravans or trailers, offering strong engines and reassuring stability.

As for running costs, a Tdi diesel Discovery isn't particularly expensive to drive, although what was excellent fuel economy in 1989 isn't quite so spectacular today. A petrol V8 Discovery is a superb machine, with better road performance than the diesels, but you'll pay for it at the petrol pumps. Where diesels can average 30mpg (a lot depends on the type of use they get), the V8 is more likely to settle at about 18mpg, maybe nearer 14mpg if it's an automatic. The Mpi averages 23mpg, and with worse performance than the V8s it's not a logical alternative to either the V8s or the Tdi diesels.

The Discovery has excellent off-road ability, with superb axle articulation, permanent four-wheel drive, and a low range set of crawler gears.

Nobody would ever describe a Discovery's performance as thrilling, even with the V8. You can't throw one about like a modern car, even if it's a later model with anti-roll bars. Expect clunks in the driveline because there are a lot of joints where slack has to be taken up, and you'll soon find that potholes will cause plenty of thumping from the tyres and a bumpy (even if well controlled) ride. Discoverys

The CD stacker, when fitted, is under the passenger seat, and the seat base cover has to be removed to gain access to it.

The towing ability is excellent, thanks to good low-range torque. Mpi models are lacking in this respect.

are also noisier than many modern cars, and you will probably have to get used to a certain amount of transmission whine.

Don't expect the average person to recognise a Discovery as a classic vehicle in the same way that he might see a Mercedes-Benz SL from the same era. The Discovery was never glamorous and never intended to be, even though ownership conferred a certain cachet when they were new.

One day, the Discovery may be seen as a classic design – to many of those who understand the motor industry, it already is – but at the time of writing there are still too many in everyday use, and too many in rough condition; time will tell.

As for looking after a Discovery, there are many specialists who can do the job for you, competently and without charging a fortune. However, don't expect village garages to be able or willing to carry out the more complex jobs. A Discovery isn't an average saloon car, and specialist knowledge can be a necessity. There are many ways a Discovery differs from the cars your local garage owner sees all the time.

Having said that, don't be afraid to look after your Discovery yourself. Routine servicing isn't difficult, as long as you have a decent workshop manual and the appropriate tools. Buy the parts manual for your model too. The ones produced by Land Rover contain diagrams that are very useful for DIY mechanics. The best compromise is to do as much as possible yourself, then find a local specialist who will help you out when you run into difficulties, or take on the trickier jobs for you.

Finally, never forget that your Discovery has superb off-road ability, and many enthusiasts buy them primarily so that they can enjoy taking advantage of this. A tow bar will typically reduce your departure angle (the angle at which you can drive up a slope without catching the rear of the vehicle on the ground), but even then, chunky tyres and two-inch suspension lifts aren't necessary unless you aim to do some really extreme stuff: a Discovery is that good.

The amount of light from the twin glass sunroofs and rear Alpine lights makes the rear seat appear more spacious than it really is. This is an early three-door model, and the seats are fitted with optional waterproof covers.

The seven-seat models can indeed carry seven people, but the rearmost occasional seats are best reserved for children. The large pouch visible behind the rear seat in this picture is a zip bag for the early removable sunroof panel.

The Discovery's characteristic binnacle-mounted control switches are unusual, but quite logical once you are used to them.

Not every Discovery came with this roller-blind cover for the rear load area, but it's a worthwhile extra that conceals the contents.

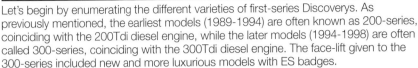

Let's begin by enumerating the different varieties of first-series Discoverys. As previously mentioned, the earliest models (1989-1994) are often known as 200-series, coinciding with the 200Tdi diesel engine, while the later models (1994-1998) are often called 300-series, coinciding with the 300Tdi diesel engine. The face-lift given to the 300-series included new and more luxurious models with ES badges.

Breaking down these major varieties into sub-types, we have three-door models (throughout), and five-door models (1990-1998). Both the 200- and 300-series were available with five or seven seats.

Most Discoverys were ordered with a diesel engine, which means either 200Tdi or 300Tdi. A manual gearbox was the main option, either the LT77 (1989-1994) or R380 (1994-1998). Automatic gearboxes were available from 1994.

The early three-door models were distinguished by large side decals and styled steel wheels.

There were two types of petrol engine. Least common was the 2-litre Mpi (1992-1997), with manual gearbox only. Much more numerous was the V8, which was the only one available on NAS (North American Specification) models. There were four different versions of the V8: carburettor 3.5-litre (1989-1990); injected 3.5-litre (1990-1993); injected 3.9-litre (1993-1998); and some late NAS models had the 4-litre V8, which had the same swept volume as the 3.9-litre.

There was a van (commercial) model as well, based on the three-door Discovery. This one is a face-lift model.

The early three-door models, with their distinctive side decals, have something of a cult following, but at the time of writing aren't fetching big money. In all honesty, they're much more crude and much less practical than the five-door models, the best of which are probably the later model ES types, with all the extra toys and equipment.

The face-lift models brought a redesigned nose and a rather more substantial look. This 1996 model has the XS specification, which was a cosmetic package of decals and special upholstery.

Five-door models generally had less garish decals; this one was sold in France. Most have alloy wheels as well.

As far as engines are concerned, the 300Tdi is probably the best – relatively frugal, relatively refined, strong and durable. From 1996, the 300Tdi automatics had extra power and torque to raise performance levels. The V8 is a lovely engine in all its forms, but its thirst puts off many buyers. The Mpi gets bad press, and its fuel consumption is disappointing, but it's actually a fine engine if you don't need low-down torque for towing.

Diesels are the most sought-after; this is an early 200Tdi.

The V8 petrol engine is delightful but thirsty. The carburettor version pictured here was sold for one year only.

The V8 grew to 3.9 litres, and in this size always came with fuel injection.

The favourite Discovery engine is the 300Tdi diesel, used after March 1994. Note the additional soundproofing.

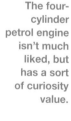

The four-cylinder petrol engine isn't much liked, but has a sort of curiosity value.

Left: There were different configurations of the side decals for some markets, and they also varied over the years in Britain.

Bottom Left: Multiple special-edition Discoverys were available over the years; this is an Argyll three-door from 1998. Most had various combinations of optional equipment, but they're otherwise not especially desirable – except to a hardcore Discovery enthusiast.

5 Before you view

– be well informed

To avoid a wasted journey, and the disappointment of finding a Discovery that does not match your expectations, you should be very clear about what you want to ask before picking up the phone. Some of these points might seem basic, but the excitement of buying your dream classic can very easily allow the most obvious things to slip the mind ... Also check the current values of your chosen model in classic car magazines, which give a price guide and auction results.

Where is the car?

Is it going to be worth travelling to the next county, state, or even across a border? Viewing a locally advertised car, even if it may not exactly fit your needs, can provide you with better knowledge for future viewing, with very little effort – it could even be better than you expected.

Dealer or private sale

Establish early on if the car is being sold by its owner or by a trader. A private owner should have all the history, so don't be afraid to ask detailed questions. A dealer may have limited knowledge of a car's history, but should have documentation, and may offer a warranty/guarantee (ask for a printed copy) and finance.

Cost of collection and delivery

A dealer may be able to give a quote for delivery via car transporter. A private owner might meet you halfway, but only agree to this after you have seen the car at the vendor's address to validate the documents. Conversely, you could meet halfway to agree the sale, but insist on meeting at the vendor's address for the handover.

View – when and where

It's preferable to view at the vendor's home or business premises. With a private sale, the documentation should match the vendor's name and address. Arrange to view in daylight, and avoid a wet day. Cars can look better in poor light or when wet.

Reason for sale

Make this one of the first questions. Why is the car being sold? How long has it been with the current owner? How many previous owners?

Left-hand drive to right-hand drive

If a steering conversion has been done it can only reduce the value, and it may be that other aspects of the car still reflect a foreign specification. However, you will very rarely find this on a Discovery in the UK.

Condition (body/chassis/interior/mechanicals)

Ask for an honest appraisal of the car's condition. Ask specifically about some of the quick evaluation items described later in chapter 7.

All original specification

A car that is wholly original is invariably of higher value than a customised version.

Matching data/legal ownership

Do VIN/chassis, engine numbers and licence plate match the official registration document? Is the owner's name and address recorded in the official registration documents?

For those countries that require an annual test of roadworthiness (an MoT certificate in the UK, which can be verified on 0300 123 9000 or gov.uk/check-mot-status), does the car have a document showing it complies?

If a smog/emissions certificate is mandatory, does the car have one?

If required, does the car carry a current road fund licence/licence plate tag?

Does the vendor own the car outright? Money might be owed to a finance company or bank: the car could even be stolen. Several organisations will supply the data on ownership, based on the car's licence plate number, for a fee. Such companies can often also tell you whether the car has been written-off by an insurance company. In the UK these organisations can supply vehicle data via their websites or on these numbers:

DVSA – 0800 123 9000   DVLA – 0300 790 6802
HPI – 01722 413 434   RAC – 0330 159 0364
AA – 0800 316 3564

Other countries will have similar organisations.

Unleaded fuel

All petrol (gasoline) Discoverys should be able to run on unleaded fuel without modification.

Insurance

Check with your existing insurer before setting out; your current policy might not cover you to drive the car if you do purchase it.

How you can pay

A cheque will take several days to clear and the seller may prefer to sell to a cash buyer. A banker's draft (a cheque issued by a bank) is as good as cash, but safer, so contact your bank and become familiar with the formalities necessary to obtain one.

Buying at auction?

If the intention is to buy at auction, see chapter 10 for further advice.

Professional vehicle check (mechanical examination)

There are often marque/model specialists who will undertake professional examination of a vehicle on your behalf. Owners' clubs will be able to put you in touch with such specialists. Other organisations in the UK that will carry out a general professional check are:

AA – 0800 056 8040 (motoring organisation with vehicle inspectors)
ABS – 01925 287 300 (specialist vehicle inspection company)
RAC – 0330 159 0364 (motoring organisation with vehicle inspectors)

Other countries will have similar organisations.

6 Inspection equipment
– these items will really help

Before you rush out of the door, gather a few items that will help as you work your way around the Discovery.

This book
Reading glasses (if you need them for close work)
Magnet (not powerful, a fridge magnet is ideal)
Torch
Probe (a small screwdriver works very well)
Overalls
Mirror on a stick
Digital camera
A friend, preferably a knowledgeable enthusiast

This book is designed to be your guide at every step, so take it along and use the check boxes to help you assess each area of the car. Don't be afraid to let the seller see you using it.

Take reading glasses (if you need them) to read documents and carry out close up inspections.

A magnet will help you check if the car is full of filler, or has fibreglass panels. Use the magnet to sample bodywork all around the car, but be careful not to damage the paintwork. Expect a little filler here and there, but not whole panels. There's nothing wrong with fibreglass panels, but a purist might want the Discovery to be as original as possible.

A torch with fresh batteries will be useful for peering into the wheelarches and under the vehicle.

A small screwdriver can be used – with care – as a probe, particularly in the wheelarches and on the underside. You should be able to check an area of severe corrosion, but be careful – if it's really bad the screwdriver might go right through the metal!

Be prepared to get dirty. Take a pair of overalls, if you have them. Having a mirror on a stick will enable you to check the condition of the Discovery's underside, and help you to peer into some of the important crevices. You can also use it, together with the torch, along the underside of the sills and on the floor.

If you have access to a digital camera, take it along so that later you can study areas of the car more closely. Take photos of parts of the car that cause you concern, and seek a friend's advice.

Ideally, have a friend or knowledgeable enthusiast accompany you: a second opinion is always valuable.

7 Fifteen minute evaluation
– walk away or stay?

There's one more thing you should do before you set off to look at a potential purchase. Having found out from the seller what type of Discovery it's supposed to be (say, a 1993 five-door Tdi), make sure you know what specification to expect. You can find this out using some of the books listed on page 60. It's very easy to modify or upgrade a Discovery by adding non-original wheels, more modern seats, or even a different engine. All these things will detract from the value of a vehicle, and may make it worthless to somebody who wants one in original condition. If such modifications don't bother you, and make the vehicle closer to what you want, then go ahead with the inspection.

You can often draw some conclusions from the location of the vehicle. Tough neighbourhood? Farmyard? Back-street dealer? Neat suburban drive? These can tell you things about a Discovery that the seller won't mention. Form your own opinion.

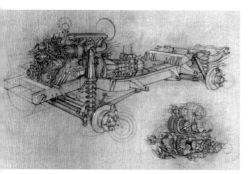

Before looking at a Discovery, it's a good idea to have some idea of how it's constructed. This publicity drawing shows the sturdy chassis frame, and, bottom right, the complex gear train.

This is the part of a Discovery you can't see – the steel inner body shell, pictured in this case with the roof welded to the steel hoops that support it.

Exterior

The first stage when checking a potential purchase is to have a good look round the outside of the vehicle. Does it sit square, or lean to one side? Are there scrapes and dents on the panels? What about the paintwork? Is the glass in good condition, or are there chips and cracks in the windscreen?

You can get a good indication of the overall condition of a Discovery by looking at the bumper end caps. Plenty of scrapes will indicate some careless use. Have a look for damage at the front apron spoiler as well; this is another useful indicator. Check the body panels for signs of corrosion, especially low down on the rear wings ahead of the wheels on three-door models, and at the bottom of the tail door.

What condition are the wheels in? Alloys suffer from kerbing damage and corrosion. What about the tyres? Make sure they are radials of the correct size and speed rating; it isn't unheard of for sellers to put cheaper van tyres on the vehicle.

Rust can appear in the most unlikely places: this is the leading edge of the roof, which is made of steel.

The green mould makes clear that this Discovery has stood for some time. Surprisingly, the bumper end-cap is in good condition.

Kerbing damage around the rim means that this alloy wheel will need to be properly refurbished.

If this is what greets you when you get there, expect the worst!

Under the bonnet

You'll probably already know which engine to expect, but it's worth remembering that a few Discoverys have been fitted with non-standard diesel engines for economy reasons. If at this point you find out that it has a Daihatsu engine, have a good think about whether that's what you want from a Discovery. Remember, too, that your insurer may ask to see an engineer's report before agreeing to cover the vehicle.

Next, what is the general condition of the engine bay? Remember that the Discovery is supremely competent off-road, and may have been used as such. Even if it has only been used once in wet and muddy conditions, it's likely that mud will have been thrown into the engine bay and stuck there. Not many owners go to the trouble of steam-cleaning the engine, so a muddy or sandy engine bay will tell its own story.

A slightly grubby engine bay might be described as good and honest; layers of dust and oil vapour settling on the components aren't often cleaned, and shouldn't be a cause for concern. However, if the whole engine bay seems oily, suspect problems such as oil leaks; the Tdi diesels often have a leaky rocker cover gasket.

Check the level and colour of the oil. This will give you an idea of whether the vehicle has been serviced recently or not – you can compare your own impression with what the seller tells you. Checking the coolant in the header tank will give you a further indication of how well the vehicle has been looked after. Coolant with a milky appearance, or a film of oil in the filler neck, might point to head gasket trouble. On the 300Tdi, look out for water leaking down the block behind the alternator: it could be a failed gasket (called a P gasket).

A good engine in its day was the Mazda four-cylinder diesel – but do you want a standard engine?

Have a look at the ignition leads on the petrol engines. Are they all clipped into plastic guides, or loose and lying on the engine? What about other wiring: to the washer bottle, or (on some models) the level gauge on the header tank? Frayed wiring and corroded terminals mean trouble is lying in wait. Then have a look at the condition of the auxiliary belts. Is the fan belt tight? It may be over-tight if it has been specially adjusted in time for your visit.

Start the engine, or ask the seller to do so. Does it start easily, or is there a lot of churning first? Don't worry too much if injected V8s hunt or stumble at first: most do that before quickly settling down. Is there smoke from the exhaust on start-up? How does the engine sound as it idles? With the bonnet open, any untoward noises that may be masked during a test drive can become much more apparent.

Underneath

It's easy to check the underside of a Discovery because of the vehicle's high ground clearance. Protect your clothes with a blanket or overalls and crawl under.

You are looking for two separate things. One is the condition of the chassis frame and axles. The other is the condition of the body's underside. The chassis frame is tough and rugged, but the body suffers terribly, so expect some problems. If you see none, it's either an exceptional vehicle, or you haven't looked hard enough.

The chassis frame's weaknesses are mainly at the rear. Water, mud and stones get thrown onto the rear sidemembers, and can become trapped between the chassis and the body. Here,

The rear bumper has been removed here to show the body rear crossmember. Normally, you'll have to feel behind the bumper to assess its condition.

they can start corrosion that may go undetected for years. Have a good feel on top of the chassis sidemembers, especially near the rear axle. Tap the chassis with something like a coin if you're not sure: good metal gives a clear metallic ringing noise, but corroded metal returns a dull thud.

Look carefully for signs of welding. Weld repairs themselves aren't a bad thing – at least somebody has been looking after the vehicle – but cheap repairs are often done by welding sheet

Yes, it's only cosmetic, but do you want the trouble of sorting it out before it gets worse?

metal over corroded areas and then plastering it with thick underseal. It's better to see areas where the original chassis paint has flaked off than to see the whole chassis caked in a thick compound that prevents you from looking at the metal underneath. If there's lots of underseal, use your screwdriver to feel around and get an idea of what it's covering. If there's plenty of Waxoyl or a similar protective compound, at least one of the vehicle's owners has tried hard to keep it in good order.

As far as the body is concerned, there are three areas to look at. Most obvious is the splash-plates behind the rear wheels. They're not integral to the structure, but are very vulnerable and do rot through, sometimes leaving the rear mudflaps with no mounting point. Problems here make a good bargaining point.

You should also look at the body sills, which can be found at the outboard lower edge of the body, as the strength of the body and the outboard body-to-chassis mounting points depends on them; weak or rotten sills are an immediate roadworthiness test failure on structural grounds.

The major area of concern is the body's rear crossmember. Located right at the back of the vehicle, it gets bombarded by whatever the rear wheels throw at it, and suffers accordingly. As the crossmember carries body-to-chassis mounting points, problems here will also lead to roadworthiness failure.

On the inside

Check the condition of the headlining. Almost every Discovery will suffer from a leaking roof at some point, and will often stain the headlining. Also see if it has begun to part company with its backing pad and sag. Look around the top of the windscreen and sunroof openings. The Alpine lights at the rear are notorious for leaking, but the plastic trim disguises this. Look around the rubber seals for any issues, and lower down the body sides for signs of dampness.

What is the condition of the front carpets? A leaking windscreen can allow water to get under the carpets, where it will sit for years, gradually causing the steel floor to rot through. Even if there's nothing to see, check under the carpets, too, to see if water is trapped between the underfelt and metal floor but has not yet penetrated the carpets.

A quick check of the seats will reveal quite a lot: a grubby appearance suggests that the Discovery has not been very well looked after. Look for wear on the outboard edge of the driver's seat. Oddly, it's often simpler to replace worn leather panels than similar ones in all-fabric upholstery.

If there's a metal strip on the dash, don't worry. Early face-lift models had a peculiar fault where the edge of the dash by the windscreen would start to lift. Better glue cured this by 1996, but there was a factory 'fix' which involved screwing a metal strip to the dash to hold it down.

If the Discovery has air-conditioning, check that it blows cold air when engaged; if not, a new compressor is expensive.

You should also take a look at the plastic trim, which can crack and eventually break, especially the door bins; don't forget to check the one on the tail door, and look at the plastic strip that holds the carpet of the rear loadspace in place – it's often broken.

Special editions

It's beyond the scope of this book to go into the minutiae of the special-edition Discoverys. You'll either need to take an expert along, or be very certain of what you expect before you view a vehicle. However, bear in mind that Land Rover often created special editions by adding accessories to otherwise basic models to boost sales at the bottom end of the Discovery range; they're not all laden with exotic options. Buyers generally assess special editions on their overall level of equipment rather than on their rarity; don't be tempted to pay over the odds.

How does it go/sound/feel?

You should take the Discovery for a short test drive before going away to think about what you've seen.

Twin sunroofs are a mixed blessing, so have a thorough look for leaks!

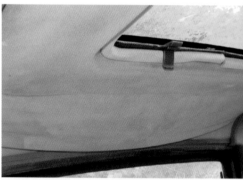

Leaks are a major cause of sagging headlinings, like this rear section.

Signs of hard use ... you can assume that there will have been other, less visible damage as well. The grille, by the way, seems to be a special Gulf States version.

Remember that you will need to be insured to drive it and not every insurance policy covers you in somebody else's vehicle. You should also check that the vehicle is road legal; if you take a test drive on a public road in a vehicle without a valid roadworthiness certificate, you will be breaking the law.

The 200Tdi engine may sound alarmingly tractor-like (although considered pretty good in its day), while the combustion noise from the later 300Tdi should be much better suppressed. Turbocharger boost shouldn't be too noticeable as it cuts in, and there shouldn't be a sudden transition; check through the rear window for black smoke when accelerating; any smoke could be from wear in the injection system, or a turbocharger problem. The V8 engines should pull cleanly and smoothly, although there may be some top-end clatter from a worn valve-gear.

Does it run in a straight line if you take your hands very briefly off the wheel? Does it pull up in a straight line when you brake? On models with ABS, check that the dashboard warning light comes on when you turn the key, and goes out when you reach about 5mph; it's not unknown for an ABS fault to be disguised by removing the warning light bulb.

Expect a certain amount of driveline shunt; even the late top-spec automatics may clunk noticeably when put into gear from neutral. However, if that clunk is very metallic, there's wear somewhere. Expect more clunks and bangs in the driveline, as the drive is taken up and on the overrun; but keep in mind, the more severe these are, the more wear is present. Expect some gear whine from the transfer box, too, although this should be background noise, not intrusive.

With manual gearboxes, listen for gears that chatter on the overrun, and make sure that all gears can be selected, including reverse. Check that second and third do not jump out of engagement on the overrun. With automatics, the changes should be smooth both up and down the gearbox, if not, there's a problem. Slurring on upchanges indicates wear.

The transfer box lever can seize up if unused for long periods. So select low ratio, and engage the differential lock. Drive a short distance with the differential locked, but remember that using diff lock on sealed surfaces can cause tyre wear. When you disengage the differential lock, you'll need to drive a few more yards before the warning light goes out.

Paperwork
Lastly, take a look at the paperwork. Is the seller's name on the documentation? Do the chassis and engine numbers match those on the vehicle? How long has the seller owned it? Problem vehicles are often sold on very quickly.

If the vehicle has been modified significantly, check that these modifications have the approval of local authorities. In some countries, what you can do to a vehicle (for example, to improve its off-road ability) is limited by legislation.

Rust in the roof again – this would be tricky and costly to repair.

8 Key points
– where to look for problems

Once you've been for a preliminary viewing, you'll want to spend some time thinking over what you've seen before deciding whether to go for a second look – which is what the next chapter is all about.

First, you'll need to sort out the mass of information you've just gathered, so that you can begin to make some sense of it. Start by focusing on some key points:
• Is the vehicle structurally sound?
• Is it cosmetically acceptable?
• Does the engine seem good?

If you answer 'yes' to all these questions, you're likely to want another more detailed look. If you answer 'no' to any question, chances are that you'll give this one a miss.

If you're thinking of taking another look, here are a few more deal-breaker questions first:
• How much work will you have to do to make it meet your standards?
• Is it *really* the Discovery you want? For example, is it a five-seater when you really wanted a seven-seater?
• Are you going to have to do some tricky explaining to your wife/husband/significant other when you get it home?

If you've been honest when answering these questions and are still interested in the vehicle, move on to the next chapter.

Somebody has taken care with this one: tail door hinges can sag, and this one has been replaced, although not painted to match the body.

The lacquer coat is peeling off the paint here. It won't stop the Discovery from running okay, but it looks scruffy. Can you put up with it until you get it repainted?

The corroded panel, the damaged window seal, and the broken guttering give an impression of neglect. Can you risk finding other evidence of neglect?

This is another potential deal-breaker. The leather seat covering has dried out, cracked, and split. You might be able to tolerate it, but are you the only one who will drive the vehicle?

It's the right engine (a 200Tdi diesel), but it looks a bit oily and neglected. Think carefully before deciding to go ahead with a deal.

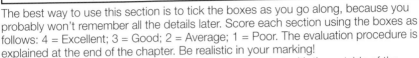

9 Serious evaluation
– 60 minutes for years of enjoyment

The best way to use this section is to tick the boxes as you go along, because you probably won't remember all the details later. Score each section using the boxes as follows: 4 = Excellent; 3 = Good; 2 = Average; 1 = Poor. The evaluation procedure is explained at the end of the chapter. Be realistic in your marking!

The inspection sequence follows a logical order: start with the outside of the vehicle; move on to the interior; then examine the engine bay and the underside. If inspecting a vehicle at a dealership or specialist's premises, ask if you can use a hoist or ramp to make inspecting the underside easier. The final stage is to take a test drive.

Paintwork and decals

Low-specification Discoverys tended to be painted with 'solid' colours, while the metallics, available at an extra cost, were typically found on better-equipped models. Check for signs of touching-in and repainting, especially if the surface below feels uneven; the new paint may be covering aluminium corrosion (see overleaf). It isn't easy to get a good paint match for metallic colours when partially respraying a panel, and it will usually be obvious if this has been done. You can use it as a bargaining point.

Paint blemishes are less easy to detect under the decals used on early three-door models – and there are lots of decals! Most have been unobtainable for many years, so replacement will involve having some specially made.

Special editions are only really as valuable as the extra equipment they have, but note that replacing a damaged special edition decal like this one will again mean getting one made specially.

Bull bars were a common accessory when these Discovery models were new, and this wrap-around style was actually a Land Rover-approved accessory. Steel bull bars of this style may now be illegal where you live: check local regulations. They can be removed easily enough, but may leave awkward scars.

On many early Discoverys, the flanks had large decal strips. For the most part, these are now unobtainable, so if they're damaged on this Discovery, decide whether to remove them altogether, which could cause paint damage, or replace them. Replacement will probably involve getting a specialist to scan the originals and make up new ones, so budget accordingly.

Discoverys were often fitted with light guards. Depending on how carefully these were fitted, the panelwork around their mountings may have corroded quite badly, so check this area.

The body

4 3 2 1

Panel fit on Discoverys was generally quite good, and certainly better than on early 1990s Range Rovers. Serious panel misalignment should ring alarm bells, because it suggests poorly repaired accident damage.

Most of the Discovery's outer panels are made from aluminium alloy, which doesn't rust but can corrode. The telltale signs are bubbling paint and traces of white powder underneath it. Bear in mind, too, that the aluminium alloy is quite soft and easily dented.

This sort of damage to paint around the rear guttering is a clear sign of neglect. The rear washer nozzle is missing here, too.

Front wings/fenders

Front wings are well protected from damage by the wraparound bumper, but do check for corrosion at their bottom edges, and feel around inside the wheelarches too. An optional extra was a set of black side protectors, which fit above the wheelarches and continue over the doors to the back of the vehicle. Check that these aren't hiding problems in the metal underneath.

Bonnet

The bonnet panel on Discoverys is usually a good fit, so if there are uneven gaps between the bonnet and the front wings, it's possible accident damage has pushed things out of line. The panel doesn't often corrode, but have a good look right at the nose, above the grille, for stone chips that could turn into rust spots later.

A common problem is that the rear step seizes on its pivot. Check that it moves easily, and returns to this position.

Doors

Doors should all be a good fit; if they aren't, there's something wrong. They have steel inners and aluminium outer skins, so take a good look where the outer skin has been folded over the frame – right at the bottom, and on the leading and trailing edges. Where the two metals meet, electrolytic reactions can lead to corrosion of the aluminium alloy, and the steel will start to rust too.

This sort of damage isn't common but is easy to miss without a close look. The plastic tread plate on the rear bumper is cracked.

The window frames are also worth checking. These are made of steel and can start to rust if the black surface coating is damaged. Look particularly at the points where they enter the lower door sections; a build-up of rainwater here can promote rusting.

Does the central locking work? Make sure it locks and unlocks *all* the doors. Door lock problems are quite common on Discoverys.

Roof panel & sunroof (if fitted)

4 3 2 1

The roof panel is hard to get to, but if you have something to stand on you should certainly try. Because it's hard to reach, owners often don't clean it, and you may find a build-up of green deposits, especially around the gutters and the sunroof.

If the gutters have been damaged, the vehicle has probably had a roof rack at some stage. Check the roof itself too, because the steel will rust if the protective layers of paint have been damaged.

Expect a certain amount of corrosion on the roof bars when fitted. They're made of aluminium alloy and will begin to corrode as soon as the black protective paint gets damaged and starts to flake off.

Sunroofs were a very common feature on Discoverys, and many vehicles had two of them. There are manually-operated and electric types, and both can seize through lack of use. Check that they open and close properly. On electric sunroofs, the motor can burn out if the sunroof has seized.

Sunroofs are great for letting more light in, but are prone to regular leaking. If they have been leaking, stains on the headlining will make it obvious. Don't be surprised to find mastic around the edges, where a frustrated

This side step was photographed when brand new, but over the years many have suffered from impact damage or corrosion.

This is typical, if bad, corrosion along the lower edge of the rear wheelarch panel.

owner has tried to seal them permanently shut!

Sills/rockers, side-steps

The steel body rails, or sills, that run under the doors are hard to see thanks to the deep plastic covers. However, it would be wise to take a closer look if you find bad corrosion in the outer edges of the floor (see below), where it meets these rails. If necessary, repair is likely to be tricky and time-consuming.

Many Discoverys were fitted with side steps (to help smaller people get into the tall vehicle) or with side runners, which were typically a cosmetic addition. Both are bolted to the chassis outriggers that support the body, and both are vulnerable to damage. As it takes a pretty hard knock to bend such large and solid pieces of metal, keep an eye out for other damage. If a step or side runner is damaged on one side, it might be difficult to get a replacement to match, especially if the item is aftermarket rather than supplied by Land Rover.

Rear body sides

On both three-door and five-door Discoverys, the rear lower panels are part of pressings that include the upper body

Even the front face of the rear wheelarch can hole through corrosion.

The seam at the top of each rear wheelarch (this is a five-door model) can rust badly.

More rear wheelarch corrosion, and it's clear here how the carpet will conceal rust that has reached as far as the belt mounting point.

sides as well. The longer panels on the three-door models are prone to corrosion at their lower edges, and to a much greater degree than the shorter panels on five-doors. On all models, look at the area behind the rear wheels, and especially at the flange at the lower edge of the body. You might find corrosion; you might find damage sustained during an off-road excursion. On bad examples, the rear inner panels can also rust.

In this case, the corrosion has been crudely covered up by the application of body filler. It's a structural problem that will lead to refusal of a roadworthiness certificate.

The lower D-posts

[4] [3] [2] [1]

If you're looking at a five-door Discovery, open the rear doors and examine the leading faces of the rear wheelarches that are now exposed. They may show signs of rust, especially around the lower mounting points for the outboard rear seatbelts. Unsurprisingly, this will lead to a roadworthiness test failure.

Water leaking from sunroofs or windscreens can cause this kind of problem in the front footwells. It's invisible unless you lift the carpet.

On a three-door model, it's harder to see the problem; you'll have to get into the back seat and pull up the carpet around the belt mounting points. The seller may not be very enthusiastic about you doing this, but it's obvious that you need to know the state of the metalwork.

Footwells and floors

[4] [3] [2] [1]

Water leaking from a failed windscreen seal may collect in the front footwells. Wet carpets are a good indication that this has happened, but it's advisable to lift the footwell carpets and check underneath as well. You may find rust in the toeboards (the angled section ahead of the floor itself), in the outer edges where they meet the inner side panels, and on the backs of the front wheelarches. If there's rust there, check the inner wings carefully when you take a look under the bonnet later.

You'll want to get a closer look at the floor in the rest of the passenger cabin, and will ideally need to get the seller's permission to lift those carpets; they tuck under the kick-plates on the sills and can be gently levered out. However, if the carpet is threadbare, or worse, wet, you'll need to be very careful not to do more damage to it. It's rare to find a Discovery with no signs of rust at the outer edges of the floor, but if you discover serious rust there you're looking at expensive trouble. Repairs will involve stripping much of the interior out (so that it doesn't catch fire during welding), and the rust may have spread to the body sills as well, adding further welding and expense.

The tail door release is concealed behind this moulding. It can sometimes fail, leaving the door impossible to open from the outside.

Tail door

The tail door makes the Discovery a highly practical vehicle, but it's also the source of several problems. It's big, and made heavy by the spare wheel hung on it. That added weight is increased further by things such as the optional metal wheel cover, and tools and other clutter that owners carry in the inside pocket. Unsurprisingly, it tends to drop on its hinges. If it drags against the lower edge of the opening, then that's what's happened. It's possible that the hinges have worked a little loose, but it's easy enough to tighten their bolts.

Look particularly at the bottom right-hand corner of the door. The alloy skin

The matching spare wheel cover is an attractive accessory, but check for paint chips and similar damage.

This sort of corrosion on the tail door is very common, and is tricky to put right.

is folded over the steel frame, and as this is a fairly inaccessible spot, it rarely gets cleaned. As a result, it's very likely that you will find aluminium corrosion here. It will cause the bottom of the steel inner frame to rust, and lead to unsightly bubbling on the outer skin. Temporary cures are possible, if rather time-consuming, but the only long-term answer is to fit a new door and take good care of it, which is likely to be very expensive.

The rear door lock also needs a careful check. It very often fails to function with the rest of the central locking. The outer release handle may refuse to work, while the inner release will open the door just fine. The cause is often a simple lock spring failure, which is easy enough to fix and inexpensive, although access to do the job is tricky.

The boot floor is steel and can rot through. The best solution is to replace it completely with a new panel, as here.

Loadspace floor   4 3 2 1

The loadspace floor is another common source of problems on a Discovery. Sitting behind the rear axle and above the fuel tank, it's bombarded with mud, salt and road debris thrown up by the wheels. This will all stick like an unwanted poultice and cause the floor to rot through from underneath.

Once the floor has holed, water will certainly come through, affecting the loadspace carpet. Serious corrosion of the floor means that it

How well will this clean up? The paint on the blacked-out screen pillar does tend to deteriorate, and then give way to rust spots if it isn't regularly cleaned.

can't be used to carry loads, so beware of load liners or wooden panels, which might be covering something. There are also seatbelt mountings that pass through this floor as well; corrosion near those will lead to refusal of a roadworthiness certificate.

To check the floor, you'll have to lift that carpet. Again, ask the seller's permission, then undo the cross head screws that hold the plastic edge trim in place. Roll back the carpet to see the metal underneath. If it's bad, budget for a couple of days' labour and, of course, a new floor panel.

Windscreen frame

It's wise to check around the windscreen frame for signs of rust in the metalwork. Rust often begins underneath the rubber seal after a windscreen has been replaced, and if the new glass hasn't been adequately sealed with waterproof compound. Once it works its way out to the visible metal, the rust will be quite advanced, and may be difficult to eradicate completely.

Also have a look at the front of the roof, where

It's important to check the inner front wings very carefully. This one is holed in several places where the vertical and horizontal sections meet.

Engine bay components will conceal inner wing problems unless you look carefully. This hole might be missed during a casual inspection.

Few people will take out the battery to check the state of the inner wing, but remember that it may conceal problems.

stone chips are often left unattended because they're hard to reach; these will turn into rust spots.

The engine bay

Under the bonnet, there's more to look at than the engine and its ancillaries. It's important to check the condition of the inner wings, especially at the back where they meet the bulkhead. Your earlier examination of the back of the wheelarches may have rung alarm bells, so now's the time to confirm your suspicions. The inner wings can be replaced, but it's a time-consuming job. However, if there's really bad rot where they meet the bulkhead, the job may be much bigger, and therefore more expensive.

Just inboard of the inner wings, you should

This corrosion is at the front of the inner wing, behind the headlight. It's tricky to spot, but visible here because the headlight has been removed.

also take a look at the front suspension towers. The large cone-like structures are bolted to the chassis above the front axle, and act as anchors for the top mountings of the dampers. These towers are likely to rust around their fixing flanges at the bottom, where they're mounted to the chassis. Weak flanges are potentially dangerous; a severe shock load through the spring could cause the suspension tower to come adrift. This is most likely to occur during heavy-duty off-road driving, but you can imagine the consequences if it happened during fast road driving. Replacing the towers is a fairly straightforward job because they simply unbolt once the dampers have been removed.

It's rare to find a Discovery that doesn't have its original (or original type) engine. Most of those sold in Europe had one of the Tdi diesel engines, which are long-lasting with acceptable fuel economy. Non-original replacement engines are more

Overheating diesel engines are never a good thing, and this 200Tdi had been losing water. The problem became clear when it was dismantled: there were tiny cracks around the valve ports, marked in yellow.

likely to be found in Discoverys that started life with one of the petrol engines. Owners replaced worn-out V8s with diesels because of the V8's appalling fuel economy, and replaced the Mpi four-cylinder with diesels because that engine lacked low-down grunt.

From the early 1990s Land Rover offered a kit to convert a V8 Discovery to Tdi power, and there were versions to suit both 200Tdi and 300Tdi engines. Typically, these kits were installed by Land Rover dealers, and therefore met factory standards. However, that cost money, and the point of the conversion was usually to save money. Because of this, a few Discoverys were given non-original diesel engines. If one of these has been fitted, you'll have spotted it in your earlier preliminary evaluation, and if you've got this far, its presence presumably isn't a cause for concern. Not yet, anyway.

It's important to find out who did the conversion, and when. That will help you assess how competently the job was done, and how long the engine has lasted so far. A very important thing to consider is whether you can still get parts for it, and what special components

Once again, rust has eaten away the lower edges of the right-hand inner front wing. The only remedy is replacement of the whole panel.

(often sourced from other vehicles) might have been used. For example, radiator hoses that were readily available at the time might not be so easily available now – especially if you don't know what vehicle they came from! An expert parts man at your local motor factor may or may not be able to identify where that top hose came from. One way or the other, your local Land Rover parts specialist is unlikely to be able to help.

Now, assuming the basic checks you did in your preliminary evaluation left you

Sadly, this is not untypical of an inner front wing, although the extent of the corrosion would be hard to spot with the outer wing panel in place.

reassured that the seller has not neglected the maintenance, the next thing is to listen to the engine running.

The diesels are noisy, the 200Tdi noticeably so, especially by modern standards, even though its refinement marked a praiseworthy advance back in 1989. You are unlikely to hear any untoward noises above the general din, so suspend your disbelief until you road-test the vehicle. The petrol V8s are quieter and smoother, but they can suffer from a variety of strange noises, most of which don't indicate anything serious.

This kind of damage is visible from underneath, but only with the aid of a torch. It's the back of the right-hand inner wing, near the bulkhead.

Again, wait until you road-test the vehicle, when any serious problems will become apparent. The Mpi should sound like any ordinary four-cylinder engine, perhaps with a bit of tappet noise. The quieter it is, the better; that means it's been maintained to a decent standard.

If it's a Tdi diesel engine, ask when the cambelt was last changed. This is a regular service requirement for both Tdi engines, and it's very often neglected, especially by owners who do their own servicing. The Mpi engines also use a cambelt which requires regular changes, so ask the same question. Cambelts eventually stretch and wear, and a broken one will cause mayhem inside the engine.

If it's a V8 engine, ask when the oil was last changed, and double-check yourself by checking its colour on the dipstick. The V8s need fresh oil every 6000 miles if they're to remain in good order. Signs of thick black sludge around the oil filler cap mean that maintenance here has been neglected.

Checking under the car

As you'll know from your preliminary evaluation, you can see under a Discovery fairly easily because of its high ground clearance. That said, it's much more comfortable if the vehicle can be raised on a hoist first, so if the seller has one (and most garages do), ask if you can use it. Now's the time to examine the bits you couldn't quite see before.

Oil leaks

4️⃣ 3️⃣ 2️⃣ 1️⃣

If the Discovery is leaking oil, it will be obvious when you get underneath. Check where the oil is coming from; worn-out sealing washers on sump plugs, and axle drain plugs are often the culprits. Cracked casings that are leaking should be very obvious, and are going to be costly to replace.

If you do discover oil leaks, then you will have to assess whether the seller has tried to keep oil levels up to their correct levels despite the leaks, or has simply trusted to luck.

Chassis frame

4️⃣ 3️⃣ 2️⃣ 1️⃣

The Discovery's chassis is a sturdy ladder frame, with heavy box-section sidemembers and a number of crossmembers. This chassis frame remained essentially unchanged throughout the vehicle's production life.

Serious rust on the chassis isn't a major Discovery problem yet, although as time goes on the situation may change. However, there may be plenty of surface rust. Look for clusters of rust-coloured pin-holes, especially in the lower corners of the box-sections; water trapped inside will eventually cause the frame member to rust from the inside out. Take a very careful look at any welded patches on the chassis; only in very high quality repair work will the metal underneath have been cleaned up and de-rusted first. A welded patch means there has been a problem, and the chances are the problem will re-appear later.

Check the chassis frame above the rear axle, and take a good look behind it as well. Debris thrown up by the rear wheels can strip the paint off the sidemembers, and if unprotected, these are likely to start rusting. A bigger problem, however, is rust on top of the chassis frame, where it can't be seen. Road debris accumulates between the

This is the neat filler for an LPG installation on a 1996 V8 Discovery. Check carefully how good an LPG installation is before assuming it will be up to scratch.

sidemembers and the underside of the body, and eventually the top surface of the frame can rust through. Check for this by feeling in the gap with your fingers (wear thin gloves to protect yourself against sharp edges).

If the frame is rusty here, there's no quick remedy. The body will have to come off and you may end up replacing the entire chassis once you have assessed the extent of the damage. This is a massively time-consuming and potentially expensive job, and at the time of writing isn't worth doing; it's more sensible to look for a better Discovery.

Check that all four axle bump-stops are present; these are the rubber buffers above the axle that prevent the axle casing from coming into contact with the chassis frame over extreme bumps. They're easy enough to replace, but it's wise to check the area where they're mounted in case it's already suffering from impact damage or rust.

All Discoverys that have been used off-road in any serious capacity are likely to bear the scars on their chassis frames. Typically, the frame may strike a rock or another large object, which will leave a dent. Unless those dents are showing signs of rusting, don't worry about them – you can of course use them as a bargaining counter when trying to strike a deal with the seller.

Body rear crossmember
Just as the metal at the bottom of the body side frames can rust, so can the body's rear crossmember – only more so. Like the back of the chassis, it gets bombarded with road debris which sticks. Rusted crossmembers are quite common, and will result in failure of a roadworthiness test because they incorporate the rear body-to-chassis mountings.

The problem is that this crossmember is pretty impossible to see until the vehicle is stripped down. To get an idea of its condition, run your hand up behind the rear bumper (you'll need those gloves again), and prod the metal hard with your fingers. If it's crumbly, there's a problem; as replacing the crossmember is a skilled job, that means either your time or your money will be required.

Fuel tank, and LPG conversions
All Discoverys were fitted with a plastic fuel tank which doesn't normally give trouble. However, it's wise to check the security of its fixings, and for signs of impact damage to the steel protection plate underneath.

Special fuel tanks were available for petrol-engined Discoverys converted to run on LPG, which was a popular way of reducing fuel costs in the 1990s, even if the payback time for the installation was quite lengthy. The extra tank was normally fitted under the right-hand side behind the rear wheel, or sometimes two were fitted to the chassis rails below the doors. However, some of the less reputable converters chose the easy option and fitted an extra tank in the load bay, where it obviously reduced load capacity.

Discoverys modified to run on LPG normally retained the ability to run on petrol from the standard fuel tank as well. If an LPG system has been fitted, ask to see evidence that the system has been checked and approved as safe by an appropriate authority. Your insurers may call for an engineer's report, too.

Front and rear axles
The axle casings may show signs of off-road damage, typically around the differential

housings, because these hang lower than the rest of the casing. Severe damage is likely to lead to leaks from the differential, although these will be easy to spot.

At each end of the front axle is a chromed ball, which swivels to allow the wheels to be steered. The chromed faces should be smooth, not pitted or rusted. If sand or mud becomes trapped under the swivel seals, it will eventually scratch or erode the chrome surface so that the seal can't work effectively, and oil will begin to leak out. Oil is essential to the workings of the steering, and severe oil leaks indicate that the ball swivels (and maybe more) need to be replaced.

On the rear axle, check the security of the brake pipes that run along its casing. They will probably be held in place by plastic ties, but that is quite good enough to keep them out of harm's way.

The Discovery's long-travel coil-spring suspension allowed some quite fearsome body roll in cornering, until later models were fitted with anti-roll bars as standard, which tamed this considerably. There was also an anti-roll bar kit that could be retro-fitted to earlier Discoverys, and there were aftermarket kits from quite early on as well. Worn rubber bushes cause the anti-roll bars to lose their effectiveness; check their condition by grasping the bar firmly and trying to move it back and forth. Anything more than absolutely minimal movement indicates worn bushes.

Suspension

Long-travel coil-springs were essential to the Discovery's basic design, and they proved sturdy and reliable. It's not impossible to break one, but a broken spring will be readily visible, and should be a warning that the vehicle has probably suffered some serious abuse.

You may be looking at a Discovery that's had a suspension lift, something typically done to raise the body to improve off-road ability (although it increases body roll on the road). If you do find this, make sure that the job has been done properly because changing the distance between chassis frame and axle casings requires more alterations than many DIY modifiers think.

The suspension contains a number of rubber bushes that wear over time, and will then cause the vehicle to handle poorly. Professional testers use pry bars to check for movement between suspension components, and you might do the same. Check the bushes on the rear radius arms and the front 'C-spanner' arms especially: movement equals wear. Some owners replace worn bushes with harder Polybushes, which come in various grades of firmness. There are other joints in the steering to check, too (see overleaf).

Brakes

All Discoverys have disc brakes on all four wheels, the front pair ventilated on most models after 1993. These give superb stopping power when in good order. Check that the correct discs are fitted, and that they aren't scored or rusty; rust works its way inwards from the outboard edge of a disc. Aftermarket cross-drilled discs are available and do a good job as replacements.

The handbrake operates on a drum directly behind the transfer gearbox. It locks movement of the rear propshaft, but, of course, can't compensate for movement in the propshaft's universal joints. This accounts for the slight lurch that often occurs on a slope before the handbrake engages, which many people find worrying. It's not unknown for the transmission brake itself to be damaged by a severe impact during off-road driving, but this sort of damage will be obvious.

Steering

4 3 2 1

Power-assisted steering was standard on Discoverys from the start, and is notorious for leaks. Major fluid leaks, from either the hydraulic pipes or the steering box, will prompt refusal of a roadworthiness certificate. Have a look at the colour and quantity of the fluid in the reservoir as an initial check; it will normally be red.

The system should not moan or hiss, although it may make protesting noises if the wheels are turned on a hard surface while the vehicle is stationary (as often happens in parking manoeuvres). If it does so in other circumstances, there's a problem.

To test for steering problems, you need to have an assistant. Ask someone to turn the steering

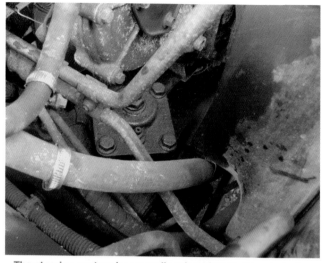

The steering system is generally robust but is prone to leaks. This one looks old but is still capable of functioning.

wheel from lock to lock while you lie under the vehicle; check for fluid leaks from the PAS box, and for movement in the steering linkages. There should be no movement at all between the swivel pin housing and the swivel steering lever at the point where they're bolted together. Free movement in any of the steering assembly's ball joints suggests wear.

Shock absorbers

4 3 2 1

It's difficult to test the shock absorbers on a Discovery using the sort of bounce test that people usually use for cars. It's also unwise, because you might dent one of the alloy panels.

Unless there are obvious fluid leaks from the dampers, or damage to their casings, wait until the road-test to assess their condition.

Propshafts

4 3 2 1

Check for wear in the transmission by grasping the front and rear propshafts in turn and trying to twist them. They will turn slightly as slack in the system is taken up, but if either rotates as much as a quarter of a turn, there's excessive wear. This may be in the differential. When testing the rear propshaft, make sure the handbrake is off in order to get a true impression.

While looking at the transmission, check for wear in the universal joints on the propshaft ends; using a screwdriver as a lever, see if there's appreciable movement between the yoke and the joint. The more movement there is, the more advanced the wear will be.

Exhaust system

The exhausts on diesel models generally last longer than those on petrol types, but you should still check the exhaust system of a Discovery Tdi thoroughly. A stainless steel system is a bonus, as it means you are unlikely to ever need a new exhaust. However, do ask to see evidence, such as an invoice, that the system really is stainless steel. It's also a good idea to check all the mountings, both rigid and flexible.

From autumn 1993, all petrol-engined Discoverys had catalytic converters in the exhaust system. There were a few about before then as well, most for countries such as (what was) West Germany, or special orders for buyers with environmental concerns. These 'cats' can be expensive to replace, and owners often try to avoid the job; check if the vehicle should have a 'cat' system and if so, whether it actually does! If the 'cat' rattles at idle when the engine is warm, it probably needs replacing. Needless to say, a vehicle originally fitted with a catalytic converter is required to have one to meet roadworthiness regulations in most countries.

While examining the exhaust, it's worth checking the tailpipe, too. On diesel models, the inside of the exhaust pipe is always likely to be a black colour. On petrol models, a light grey deposit in the pipe is a good sign, but a powdery black deposit suggests the engine is running rich, or that the vehicle has been used excessively in low-speed town traffic.

When the engine is running, steam from the exhaust of both petrol and diesel engines suggests head gasket problems (although there may be a small amount on starting a cold engine, caused by condensation in the exhaust pipe). White smoke may point to a leak from the brake servo.

Electrical system

The Discovery's electrics depend heavily on shaped plastic block connectors, which are fine when in good condition but a nightmare if they break or distort in old age. Although it's not a bad idea to check and clean connections, with these it's probably best to leave them well alone unless there's a problem.

Generally speaking, the later, and more generously equipped, a

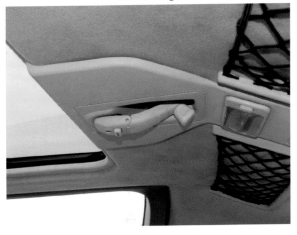

Some sunroofs are manually operated, and some use an electric motor. In either case, check for ease of opening and closing.

The later models have more electrical equipment to check. Seen on a 1993 automatic model are the electric window switches, the headlamp levelling control and the door mirror adjuster.

Discovery is, the more electrical problems it might have. However, these vehicles are average in terms of electrical faults, and the best advice is to make sure that everything electrical works; lights are a bare minimum for legal and safety reasons, but check (if fitted) the electric windows, the electric sunroof, the central locking, the electric seat adjustment and seat heaters, and even the ICE system. A radio that doesn't work shouldn't put you off buying a vehicle, but it's a bargaining point when you're trying to agree a price.

The thin-wall wiring system used on Discoverys discouraged enthusiastic DIY owners from adding non-original electrical equipment, but it's advisable to have a long and careful look at any wiring that isn't original to the vehicle, such as the power supply to a CB radio (whether or not the radio itself is still in place). It's not unknown for additional equipment to overload the original wiring and burn it out.

Test drive
You will want to take the Discovery for another test drive before deciding whether to buy it. This time, the drive will be longer, and you'll be trying harder to find the vehicle's faults.

Engine health and performance   4️⃣ 3️⃣ 2️⃣ 1️⃣
Most people assume the health of the engine is the first thing to check on a test drive, so we'll start with that, but bear in mind that it isn't always the engine that causes the most expensive problems!
• The 200Tdi and 300Tdi diesels.
Both engines should pull strongly through the gears, and still have acceleration in reserve at cruising speeds. You may find an automatic diesel is a little sluggish, which is why power and torque were improved for this drivetrain from 1996. The 300Tdi engine is much more refined than the 200Tdi, although it never lets you forget that it only has four cylinders. If there appears to be a flat spot in acceleration between about 2000rpm and 2500rpm, the diesel lift pump is probably on the way out.

Keep an eye on the engine temperature gauge. The Tdi engines are known for developing head gasket leaks and cracking cylinder heads. If the gasket has been replaced but the crack not detected, the engine is likely to overheat and will, of course, use water as well. However, you can't always tell whether a cylinder head is cracked just by driving the vehicle.

When you return from your test drive, allow the warm engine to idle for a few seconds – which is good practice because it allows the turbocharger to slow down while its oil is still circulating. Then blip the accelerator and check in the mirror for black smoke from the exhaust. If there is some, the engine is worn.

• The petrol V8s

The V8 engines should all deliver their power smoothly, although different versions have different characteristics. The sound of a healthy carburettor engine is very different from that of a late injected 3.9-litre, for example. Listen for top-end noise (the hydraulic tappets can gum up, and the camshaft can wear), and beware of misfires, which aren't always easy to detect in a multi-cylinder engine. A rough and rasping sound from one side of the engine usually means the exhaust manifold is blowing; it's unlikely to be cracked, and the remedy will probably be to tighten the manifold bolts.

• The Mpi four-cylinder

Don't expect too much of it. This is a pleasant road engine, but it lacks the low-down torque to be good for towing, and for the same reason is less able to cope with demanding off-road conditions than Discoverys with other engines. It revs higher than either the Tdi or V8 types, and there may be a variety of buzzes and zings from under the bonnet; those are quite normal.

Gearbox assessment

• Manual gearbox

There are two manual gearboxes, both five-speed. The earlier one is the LT77, which has reverse up and to the left. It gained improved synchromesh in 1992 and became the LT77S. The later, introduced in March 1994, is the R380, with reverse down and to the right. With both types, when the engine is running and in neutral, listen for the rattle that means a worn layshaft.

On the LT77 and LT77S, a deep metallic clunk as the drive takes up suggests main shaft wear. If you suspect this, confirm it by coming on and off the accelerator while driving. However, don't confuse this problem with normal wear or 'shunt' in the driveline. Wear of the main shaft will eventually lead to gear selection problems. Gear selection difficulty when the gearbox is cold usually means there's a synchromesh problem, common on second gear with the early LT77. Worn gearboxes will whine and may feel generally sloppy and loose.

The R380 also has main shaft wear and synchromesh problems, and sometimes no gear can be engaged until the gearbox has warmed up. Third gear seems to be most affected, so listen for a crunch as it's selected and as you change to second. This gearbox was deliberately designed to give slick, car-like changes, and something is wrong if it doesn't.

Both gearboxes are nonetheless capable of functioning for a very long time despite problems caused by wear. Be gentle with a worn one, and aim to fix it or replace it later.

• Automatic gearbox

The ZF automatic gearboxes are very robust and reliable. Changes are normally not very noticeable, so look out for hesitation or slurring as the box changes up; it probably means the internal clutches are worn.

Transfer gearbox

You checked that low ratio engages, and that the differential lock works properly during your preliminary evaluation. Check them both again, just to be sure.

Clutch and clutch pedal

If the clutch squeals when you push the pedal to the floor, the release bearing is probably worn. The parts aren't expensive, but fitting can be costly unless you do it yourself, which will take quite a long time. If vehicle speed doesn't increase when you press the accelerator, the clutch is worn and slipping (but refer back to the problems with the Tdi engines). Expect the clutch to bite when the pedal is about

The centre differential lock warning light should illuminate on the dash when the lock is engaged. It may not extinguish immediately after the lock is disengaged, but should do so after driving a few yards.

half-way through its travel; biting near the top or the bottom means the adjustment isn't right. Finally, if there's clutch judder as the drive is taken up, you'll need to take a closer look. Harsh gear changes that aren't down to a gearbox fault may be caused by a worn clutch fork.

Steering

The steering on a Discovery is generally well-weighted and well-suited to the vehicle. If you find that the vehicle you're testing suffers from wander, the problem is probably worn trackrod ends. If there seems to be rear-end steering in corners, the rear radius arm bushes are probably worn; check by accelerating then lifting off in a corner.

When turning the steering on a stationary vehicle, you are putting a great strain on the power assistance system, so a few groans and creaks should not be a cause for concern. However, if the steering makes similar noises on the move at low speeds, it's badly worn.

Brakes

Discovery brakes were always power assisted, and should pull the vehicle up quickly and in a straight line. On later models with ABS, loss of traction will be picked up by the ABS system, which will then pump the brakes rapidly and make a chattering noise. This is perfectly normal. The system also makes some curious moaning noises as it cycles and recharges every few minutes, but you won't normally hear those unless the vehicle is stationary with the engine running.

The handbrake operates on the transmission, so do NOT test the handbrake by applying it when the vehicle is moving. If you do, you are likely to cause some expensive damage.

Paperwork

You looked at the paperwork when you did your preliminary assessment. Now's the time to double-check that everything really is in order.

Evaluation procedure

Add up the total points, and see what category the vehicle falls into: **132 points** = Excellent; **99 points** = Good; **66 points** = Average; **33 points** = Poor.

A Discovery scoring over 93 will be completely usable and will only need regular care and maintenance to preserve its condition. A score between 69 and 92 will require a careful assessment of repair costs to reach a realistic purchase value. Cars scoring between 33 and 68 means some serious work, or even a full restoration, is needed, and this is likely to cost about the same regardless of the actual score.

10 Auctions
– sold! Another way to buy your dream

Auction pros & cons

Pros: Prices are usually lower than those of dealers or private sellers and you might get a real bargain on the day. Auctioneers have usually established clear title with the seller. At the venue you can usually examine documentation relating to the vehicle.
Cons: You have to rely on a sketchy catalogue description of condition and history. The opportunity to inspect is limited and you can't drive the car. Auction cars are often a little below par and may require some work. It's easy to overbid. There will usually be a buyer's premium to pay in addition to the auction hammer price.

Which auction?

Auctions by established auctioneers are advertised in car magazines and on auction houses' websites. A catalogue, or a simple printed list of the lots for auction, might only be available a day or two ahead, though often lots are listed and pictured on auctioneers' websites much earlier. Contact the auction house to ask if previous auction selling prices are available as this is useful information (details of past sales are often available on websites).

Catalogue, entry fee and payment details

When you purchase the catalogue of the vehicles in the auction, it often acts as a ticket allowing two people to attend the viewing days and the auction. Catalogue details tend to be brief, but will include information such as 'one owner from new, low mileage, full service history,' etc. It will also usually show a guide price to give you some idea of what to expect, and will tell you what is charged as a buyer's premium. The catalogue will also contain details of acceptable forms of payment. At the fall of the hammer an immediate deposit is usually required, and the full balance payable within 24 hours. If the plan is to pay by cash there may be a cash limit. Some auctions will accept payment by debit card. Sometimes credit or charge cards are acceptable, but will often incur an extra charge. A bank draft or bank transfer will have to be arranged in advance with your own bank as well as with the auction house. No vehicle will be released before **all** payments are cleared. If payment is delayed then storage costs can accrue.

Buyer's premium

A buyer's premium will be added to the hammer price: **don't** forget this in your calculations. It's not usual for there to be a further state tax or local tax on the purchase price and/or on the buyer's premium.

Viewing

In some instances it's possible to view lots a few days before the auction, and sometimes on the day. There are auction officials who are able to help by opening engine and luggage compartments, and allowing you to inspect the interior. While the officials may start the engine for you, a test drive is out of the question. Crawling under and around the car as much as you want is permitted, but you can't ask that the car be jacked up, or attempt to do it yourself. You can also ask to see any documentation available.

Bidding

Before you take part in the auction, **decide your maximum bid – and stick to it!**

It may take a while for the auctioneer to reach the lot you are interested in, so use that time to observe how other bidders behave. When it's the turn of your car, attract the auctioneer's attention and make an early bid. The auctioneer will then look to you for a reaction every time another bid is made; usually the bids will be in fixed increments until the bidding slows, when smaller increments will often be accepted before the hammer falls. If you want to withdraw from the bidding, make sure the auctioneer understands your intentions – a vigorous shake of the head when he or she looks to you for the next bid should do the trick!

Assuming that you are the successful bidder, the auctioneer will note your card or paddle number, and from that moment on you will be responsible for the vehicle.

If the vehicle is unsold, either because it failed to reach the reserve or because there was little interest, it may be possible to negotiate with the owner, via the auctioneers, after the sale is over.

Successful bid

There are two more items to think about. How to get the Discovery home, and insurance. If you can't drive the vehicle, a trailer (either your own or hired) is one way; another is to have the vehicle shipped using the facilities of a local company. The auction house will have details of companies specialising in the transfer of cars.

Insurance for immediate cover can usually be purchased on site, but it may be more cost-effective to make arrangements with your own insurance company in advance, and then call to confirm the full details.

eBay and other online auctions?

eBay and other online auctions could land you a Discovery at a bargain price, though you'd be foolhardy to bid without examining it first, something most vendors encourage. A useful feature of eBay is that the geographical location of the vehicle is shown, so you can narrow your choices to those within a realistic radius of home. Be prepared to be outbid in the last few moments of the auction. Remember, your bid is binding and it will be very, very difficult to get restitution in the case of a crooked vendor fleecing you – *caveat emptor*!

Be aware that some vehicles offered for sale in online auctions are 'ghost' cars. **Don't** part with **any** cash without being sure that the vehicle actually exists and is as described (usually pre-bidding inspection is possible).

Auctioneers

Barrett-Jackson www.barrett-jackson.com/
Bonhams www.bonhams.com/
British Car Auctions (BCA) www.bca-europe.com or www.british-car-auctions.co.uk/
Christies www.christies.com/

Coys www.coys.co.uk/
eBay www.ebay.com/
H&H www.handh.co.uk/
RM Sotheby's www.rmsothebys.com/
Shannons www.shannons.com.au/
Silver www.silverauctions.com

11 Paperwork
– correct documentation is essential!

The paper trail

Classic, collector and prestige cars usually come with a large portfolio of paperwork, accumulated and passed on by a succession of proud owners. This documentation represents the real history of the car and can be used to deduce the level of care the car has received, how much it's been used, which specialists have worked on it, and the dates of major repairs and restorations. All of this information will be priceless to you as the new owner, so be very wary of cars with little paperwork to support their claimed history.

Registration documents

All countries/states have some form of registration for private vehicles whether its like the American 'pink slip' system or the British 'log book' system.

It is essential to check that the registration document is genuine, that it relates to the car in question, and that all the vehicle's details are correctly recorded, including chassis/VIN and engine numbers (if these are shown). If you are buying from the previous owner, his or her name and address will be recorded in the document: this will not be the case if you are buying from a dealer.

In the UK the current (Euro-aligned) registration document is named "V5C," and is printed in coloured sections of blue, green and pink. The blue section relates to the car specification, the green section has details of the new owner and the pink section is sent to the DVLA in the UK when the car is sold. A small section in yellow deals with selling the car within the motor trade.

In the UK the DVLA will provide details of earlier keepers of the vehicle upon payment of a small fee, and much can be learned in this way.

If the car has a foreign registration there may be expensive and time-consuming formalities to complete. Do you really want the hassle?

Roadworthiness certificate

Most country/state administrations require that vehicles are regularly tested to prove that they're safe to use on the public highway and do not produce excessive emissions. In the UK that test (the 'MoT') is carried out at approved testing stations, for a fee. In the USA the requirement varies, but most states insist on an emissions test every two years as a minimum, while the police are charged with pulling over unsafe-looking vehicles.

In the UK the test is required on an annual basis once a vehicle becomes three years old. Of particular relevance for older cars is that the certificate issued includes the mileage reading recorded at the test date and, therefore, becomes an independent record of that car's history. Ask the seller if previous certificates are available. Without an MoT the vehicle should be trailered to its new home, unless you insist that a valid MoT is part of the deal. (Not such a bad idea this, as at least you will know the car was roadworthy on the day it was tested and you don't need to wait for the old certificate to expire before having the test done.)

Road licence

The administration of every country/state charges some kind of 'road licence,' a tax for the use of its roads. How this is displayed varies enormously from country to country and state to state.

Whatever the form of the 'road licence,' it must relate to the vehicle carrying it, and must be present and valid if the car is to be driven on the public highway legally. The value of the licence will depend on the length of time it will continue to be valid.

Changed legislation in the UK means that the seller of a car must surrender any existing road fund licence, and it is the responsibility of the new owner to re-tax the vehicle at the time of purchase and before the car can be driven on the road. It's therefore vital to see the Vehicle Registration Certificate (V5C) at the time of purchase, and to have access to the New Keeper Supplement (V5C/2), allowing the buyer to obtain road tax immediately.

In the UK if a car is untaxed because it has not been used for a period of time, the owner has to inform the licencing authorities, otherwise the vehicle's date-related registration number will be lost and there will be a painful amount of paperwork to get it re-registered.

Certificates of authenticity

For many makes of collectible car it is possible to get a certificate proving the age and authenticity (e.g. engine and chassis numbers, paint colour and trim) of a particular vehicle; these are sometimes called 'Heritage Certificates' and if the car comes with one of these it is a definite bonus. If you want to obtain one, the relevant owners' club is the best starting point.

If the car has been used in European classic car rallies it may have a FIVA (Federation Internationale des Vehicules Anciens) certificate. The so-called 'FIVA Passport,' or 'FIVA Vehicle Identity Card,' enables organisers and participants to recognise whether or not a particular vehicle is suitable for individual events. If you want to obtain such a certificate go to www.fbhvc.co.uk or www.fiva.org. There will be similar organisations in other countries too.

Valuation certificate

Hopefully, the vendor will have a recent valuation certificate, or a letter signed by a recognised expert stating how much they believe the particular car to be worth (such documents, together with photos, are usually needed to get 'agreed value' insurance). Generally such documents should act only as confirmation of your own assessment of the car rather than a guarantee of value as the expert has probably not seen the car in the flesh. The easiest way to find out how to obtain a formal valuation is to contact the owners' club.

Previous ownership records

Due to the introduction of important new legislation on data protection, it is no longer possible to acquire, from the British DVLA, a list of previous owners of a car you own, or are intending to purchase. This scenario will also apply to dealerships and other specialists, from who you may wish to make contact and acquire information on previous ownership and work carried out.

Service history

Often these cars will have been serviced at home by enthusiastic (and hopefully capable) owners for a good number of years. Nevertheless, try to obtain as much service history and other paperwork pertaining to the car as you can. Naturally, dealer stamps or specialist garage receipts score most points in the value stakes. However, anything helps in the great authenticity game; items like the original bill of sale, handbook, parts invoices and repair bills all add to the story and the character of the car. Even a brochure correct to the year of the car's manufacture is a useful document, and something that you could well have to search hard to locate in future years. If the seller claims that the car has been restored, then expect receipts and other evidence from a specialist restorer.

If the seller claims to have carried out regular servicing, ask what work was completed, when, and seek some evidence of it being carried out. Your assessment of the car's overall condition should tell you whether the seller's claims are genuine.

Restoration photographs
If the seller tells you that the car has been restored, then expect to be shown a series of photographs taken while the restoration was under way. Pictures taken at various stages, and from various angles, should help you gauge the thoroughness of the work. If you buy the car, ask if you can have all the photographs as they form an important part of the vehicle's history. It's surprising how many sellers are happy to part with their car and accept your cash, but want to hang on to their photographs! In the latter event, you may be able to persuade the vendor to get a set of copies made.

12 What's it worth?

– let your head rule your heart

Condition

If the Discovery you've been looking at is really bad, then you've probably not bothered to use the marking system in Chapter 9, Serious evaluation. You may not have even got as far as using that chapter at all!

If you did use the marking system in Chapter 9 you'll know whether the Discovery is in Excellent (maybe Concours), Good, Average or Poor condition or, perhaps, somewhere in-between these categories.

There were dozens of accessories for the Discovery right from the start. Not all of them sold very well, and this rather attractive grille with inset auxiliary lights remained surprisingly rare. It's interesting – but won't add to a vehicle's value.

Many specialist magazines run a regular price guide. If you haven't bought the latest editions, do so now and compare their suggested values for the model you are thinking of buying; also look at the auction prices they're reporting. Discovery values were low at the time of writing, but some models will always be more sought-after than others. Trends can change, too. The values published in the magazines tend to vary from one magazine to another, as do their scales of condition, so read carefully the guidance notes they provide. Bear in mind that a Discovery that is truly a recent show winner could be worth more than the highest scale published. Assuming that the one you have in mind isn't in show/concours condition, relate the level of condition that you judge it to be in with the appropriate guide price. How does the figure compare with the asking price?

Before you start haggling with the seller, consider what effect any variation from standard specification might have on the car's value. If you are buying from a dealer, remember there will be a dealer's premium on the price.

Desirable options/extras

Many owners consider the most desirable vehicles to be the later ones with the higher levels of equipment, such as leather or part-leather upholstery, air-conditioning, and so on. All these features certainly make it easier to live with a Discovery. Extras are much more a matter of personal preference. For example, side steps may not improve the appearance of the Discovery, but may be necessary to allow some people to get into the vehicle, which sits quite high off the ground.

Similarly, the bodykit available from 1997 is a matter of taste.

It's also worth knowing that there's a special interest in the original press launch Discoverys from 1989, known as G-WACs because they all had registration numbers in the Gxxx WAC series. (But beware; not every G-WAC was a launch vehicle!)

Undesirable features

Generally speaking, non-original features will detract from a vehicle's value – and maybe from its interest as well, if you're looking for a Discovery that's truly

By way of contrast, the ES specification on the face-lift models brings a lot of extra equipment that adds to comfort and convenience.

representative of the way they were. So avoid those with engines that were not supplied by the factory, avoid those with non-original paint schemes, and avoid those with non-original interiors.

Whether you want aftermarket accessories that were available when the Discovery was new is a matter of personal choice. Arguably, they could be considered a part of the way the vehicle was when new or nearly new, and therefore can be seen as adding value. On the other hand, some might say that if these accessories were not fitted by the factory or one of its dealers then they do not count as original.

Striking a deal

Negotiate on the basis of your condition assessment, mileage, and fault rectification costs. Also take into account the car's specification. Be realistic about the value, but don't be completely intractable: a small compromise on the part of the vendor or buyer will often facilitate a deal at little real cost.

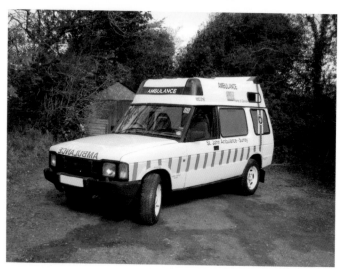

What's it worth to you? To some people, this very rare long-wheelbase ambulance conversion would be priceless, but if you just want a Discovery as everyday transport, this isn't what you need.

13. Do you really want to restore?
– it'll take longer and cost more than you think

Some people would consider restoring a Discovery from this condition, but that's not advisable unless you enjoy the restoration process and can do the work yourself. A full restoration would probably cost many times more what the finished vehicle would be worth.

What exactly do I mean by restoration? Restoring a neglected Discovery to everyday running condition is quite different from trying to get a worn-out wreck back to the way it was when it left the factory. Serious restoration demands exceptional skills and determination, plus very deep pockets. So be realistic about what you want to achieve.

Easiest of all is a rolling restoration, which means that the vehicle remains useable for most of the time, and that you improve it in larger or smaller bites as you go along. Hardest of all is what I call a resurrection, where you start with a derelict and create a viable Discovery from it.

Cost will play a very big part in what you do. It has long been a maxim in the classic car world that any restoration will take twice as long and cost at least twice as much as your original, hard-headed estimate. And don't run away with the idea that you'll be able to sell the finished restoration for more than you have spent on it. It's possible that

Restoration of major units to put an otherwise sound vehicle back into use is usually worthwhile. Here, the 200Tdi engine and automatic gearbox have been removed from a vehicle for exactly that purpose.

prices will rise that much one day, but that may be a very long time in the future. At the time of writing, people who were restoring old Discoverys were doing it for fun, not for profit.

So if you decide to restore a Discovery, restore it for yourself. Restore it to your standards, to your time-scale, and to your budget. Even if you have the skills, the equipment and the premises to do the job, resign yourself to having no free weekends for at least a couple of years. If you don't have all these vital elements and are paying somebody else to do the work, resign yourself to having no money to spend on anything else for a similar period of time: classic car restorers can, and do, charge

Restoration may involve finding missing items, and one that is often missing from early Discoverys is this detachable bag that normally lived on the centre console. This one spent many years as my camera bag.

handsomely for deploying their skills. And whichever way you decide to go, resign yourself to frustrating waits while vital parts are sourced. In a worst case, you'll have to get them re-made from scratch – that's the only way you are likely to find the early side decals, for example.

But don't let all this put you off. I'm only looking on the bleak side to ensure you think hard about what you're getting into. If you really are committed to getting that Discovery up and running and looking the way you think it should, the time, effort and money spent will all be worth it in the end. To you, at least. And after that, every little improvement will make you feel more and more proud.

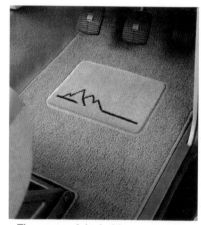

The range of desirable accessories was extensive, and included these early overmats, which are very rare to find in good condition today.

Here's another rarity that may be of interest to restorers. It's the hard plastic lockable cubby box that could replace the detachable 'handbag' on early models.

14 Paint problems

– bad complexion, including dimples, pimples and bubbles

Paint faults generally occur due to lack of protection/maintenance, or to poor preparation prior to a respray or touch-up. Some of the following conditions may be present in the car you're looking at:

Orange peel
This appears as an uneven paint surface, similar to the appearance of the skin of an orange. The fault is caused by the failure of atomized paint droplets to flow into each other when they hit the surface. It's sometimes possible to rub out the effect with proprietary paint cutting/rubbing compound, or very fine grades of abrasive paper. A respray may be necessary in severe cases. Consult a bodywork repairer/paint shop for advice on the particular car.

Cracking
Severe cases are likely to have been caused by too heavy an application of paint (or filler beneath the paint). Also, insufficient stirring of the paint before application can lead to the components being improperly mixed, and cracking can result. Incompatibility with the paint already on the panel can have a similar effect. To rectify the problem it is necessary to rub down to a smooth, sound finish before respraying the problem area.

Crazing
Sometimes the paint takes on a crazed rather than a cracked appearance when the problems mentioned under 'Cracking' are present. This problem can also be caused by a reaction between the underlying surface and the paint. Paint removal and respraying the problem area is usually the only solution.

Blistering
Almost always caused by corrosion of the metal under the paint. Usually perforation will be found in the metal and the damage will often be worse than that suggested by the area of blistering. The metal will have to be repaired before repainting.

Micro blistering
Usually the result of an economy respray where inadequate heating has allowed moisture to settle on the car before spraying. Consult a paint specialist, but usually damaged paint will have to be removed before partial or full respraying. Can also be caused by car covers that don't 'breathe'.

Fading
Some colours, especially reds, are prone to fading if subjected to strong sunlight for long periods without the benefit of polish protection. Sometimes proprietary paint restorers and/or paint cutting/rubbing compounds will retrieve the situation. Often a respray is the only real solution.

Peeling
Often a problem with metallic paintwork when the sealing lacquer becomes

damaged and begins to peel off. Poorly applied paint may also peel. The remedy is to strip and start again!

Dimples
Dimples in the paintwork are caused by the residue of polish (particularly silicone types) not being removed properly before respraying. Paint removal and repainting is the only solution.

Dents
Small dents are usually easily cured by the 'Dentmaster,' or equivalent process, that sucks or pushes out the dent (as long as the paint surface is still intact). Companies offering dent removal services usually come to your home: consult your telephone directory.

15 Problems due to lack of use

– just like their owners, Discoverys need exercise!

Cars are most efficient if they're used regularly. A run of at least ten miles, once a week, is recommended for classics.

Seized components

Pistons in calipers, slave and master cylinders can seize. The clutch may seize if the plate gets stuck to the flywheel, and pistons can seize in the bores, both due to corrosion. Handbrakes can seize if the cables and linkages rust.

Fluids

Old acidic oil can corrode bearings. Uninhibited coolant can corrode internal waterways – a particular problem with V8 engines, which have aluminium heads and block. Lack of antifreeze can cause core plugs to be pushed out, and even cause cracks in the block or head. Settled and solidified silt can cause overheating. Brake fluid should be renewed every

Lack of use may also mean that the transfer box lever (the small one) will have seized.

two years. Old fluid that's absorbed water from the atmosphere can cause corrosion and brake failure when the water turns to vapour near hot braking components.

Tyre problems

Tyres on a car that's been stationary for some time will develop flat spots, resulting in some (usually temporary) vibration. If the tyre walls have cracks or (blister-type) bulges, new tyres are needed.

Shock absorbers (dampers)

With lack of use, the dampers will lose their elasticity or even seize. Creaking, groaning and stiff suspension are signs of this problem.

Rubber and plastic

Radiator hoses can perish and split, possibly resulting in the loss of all coolant. Window and door seals can harden and leak. Gaiters/boots can crack. Wiper blades will harden.

Remember that many Discoverys have seen off-road use. If a vehicle has been left uncleaned, trapped mud and water will play havoc with the structure over periods of non-use.

Electrics

If the vehicle hasn't been used for many months, the battery will be of little use. Earthing/grounding problems are common when the connections have corroded. The electrics depend heavily on shaped plastic block connectors; unless there's a specific problem, it's wise to leave these alone. Spark plug electrodes will often corrode in an unused engine. Wiring insulation can harden and fail.

Rotting exhaust system

Exhaust gas has a high water content so exhaust systems corrode quickly from the inside when the vehicle isn't used.

16 The Community

– key people, organisations and companies in the Discovery world

The Discovery holds a special place in the hearts of Land Rover people world-wide. It lacks the luxury of a Range Rover (although top models run pretty close), and it's more family-friendly than a utility Land Rover, so many enthusiasts find that it fits the bill perfectly, as weekday transport and a weekend toy. As a result, there's plenty of specialist support around from parts suppliers and independent workshops.

The lists here are confined to the UK, but even then they're far from exhaustive. For details of clubs, specialists and suppliers in other countries, please consult your local 4x4 or Land Rover magazine, or check online.

Clubs

There are many local and regional Land Rover clubs in the UK that welcome Discoverys. However, you may find that your local club puts emphasis on off-road driving (typically green-laning), or on competitive motorsport (typically trialling), rather than on meticulous restoration for what US enthusiasts call 'show 'n' shine' events. Many clubs, of course, cater for all forms of the hobby.

Those were the days... a tempting selection of nearly-new Discoverys line up for sale at a Berkshire dealership in the early 1990s.

There is one club that is dedicated to Discoverys of all generations: the Discovery Owners' Club. You can find it on the web at: www.discoveryownersclub.org. If you're interested in joining, the membership secretary can be contacted by e-mail at: memsec@discoveryownersclub.org

Main spares suppliers

There are many suppliers of new spares for the first-generation Discovery, and this list shows only the major ones:

- **John Craddock Ltd**, North Street, Bridgtown, Cannock, Staffordshire, WS11 0AZ: 01543 577207 or www.johncraddockltd.co.uk
- **Paddock Spares and Accessories**, The Showground, The Cliff, Matlock, Derbyshire, DE4 5EW: 01629 760877, www.paddockspares.com, or sales@paddockspares.com
- **Rimmer Brothers,** Triumph House, Sleaford Road, Bracebridge Heath, Lincoln, LN4 2NA: 01522 568000, www.rimmerbros.com, or LRsales@rimmerbros.com

Specialist restorers

At the time of writing, Discovery prices were generally low, with the result that few owners were prepared to spend large sums of money on restoration or refurbishment. As a result, there was a lack of specialist restorers in the trade, and many Discovery owners relied on replacement parts sourced from scrapyards.

However, competent independent Land Rover workshops will probably be prepared to discuss major mechanical refurbishment of a Discovery. Just be sure that you agree in advance exactly what you want to be done.

Vehicle Information
If you are keen to find out the history of your own vehicle, start with the archives section of the British Motor Museum at Gaydon (01926 641188). They can normally tell you when your Discovery left the assembly

The steel road wheels tend to be favoured by those who use their Discoverys off-road; however, in the second-hand spares market, there's a higher demand for the alloy types.

lines, when it left the factory for a Land Rover dealer, who that dealer was, and also what colour it was originally. For a fee, they will provide you with a certificate that contains the available details, and is a worthwhile addition to any enthusiast's vehicle paperwork.

Magazines
• Land Rover Monthly, Dennis Publishing Ltd: www.dennis.co.uk
• Land Rover Owner International, Bauer Consumer Media Ltd: www.lro.com

Books
• *How to Modify Land Rover Discovery, Defender & Range Rover,* by Ralph Hosier. Veloce Publishing, ISBN 978-1845843151
• *You & Your Land Rover Discovery,* by Dave Pollard. Haynes Publishing, ISBN 978-1859606834
• *Land Rover Discovery 1989-1994 (Brooklands Books Road Test Series)* by RM Clarke. Brooklands Books Ltd, ISBN 978-1855202313
• *Land Rover Discovery 4x4 Performance Portfolio 1989-2000 (Brooklands Books Road Test Series)* by RM Clarke. Brooklands Books Ltd, ISBN 978-1855205598
• *Land Rover Discovery. 25 Years of the Family 4x4,* by James Taylor. The Crowood Press Ltd, ISBN 978-1847976895

There's no shortage of engines, whether straight out of a vehicle or, as in the case of this 200Tdi, carefully rebuilt to as-new condition.

17 Vital statistics
– essential data at your fingertips

Production history

It helps to understand what you're looking at if you have some idea of how the Discovery evolved during its nine years in production. So here's a breakdown of the key changes; there were very many more minor ones.

1989	Introduced as three-door model with carburettor V8 or 200Tdi diesel engines; all manual gearboxes; blue interior trim
1990	Five-door model added, also beige interior option. V8 becomes V8i with injection.
1993	V8 increased to 3.9-litre, with standard catalyst and automatic option. 2.0-litre Mpi petrol model introduced, manual only.
1994	From March (known as 1995 model-year). Face-lift models with revised front and rear ends; new dashboard incorporating airbags on some models; new upholstery on all models, and leather on the top ES model; diesel engine now 300Tdi, with automatic option; new R380 manual gearbox; anti-roll bars; ventilated front discs; ABS on top models.
1995	(NAS models only). V8 engine replaced by revised 4.0-litre type.
1996	Increased power and torque for 300Tdi engines with automatic.
1997	Mpi ends production.
1998	Last of the first-generation Discoverys built.

Chassis numbers

All Discoverys had VIN-type chassis numbers consisting of 17 digits. The last six digits were the serial number and the first 11 contain information about the specification. See Table 1 for the breakdown.

The NAS (North American Specification) codes differed slightly, as in Table 2.

Here are two examples of a Discovery VIN plate, in each case located on the bonnet locking platform. Note that the manufacturer is shown as the Rover Group (to which Land Rover then belonged), and that there are differences between them. The VIN is always shown in the second panel; the other panels are very often left blank, although in the case of the right-hand picture, they have been filled in. At the bottom left of each plate, the paint code has also been filled in.

Table 1

SAL*	Manufacturer code (Rover Group)
LJ*	Discovery
G	Standard (100-inch) wheelbase
D	Honda Crossroad (This was a rebadged Discovery, sold in Japan from 1993 to 1995)
Door Specification	
B	Three-door
M	Five-door
Engine Specification	
V	3.5-litre V8 carburettor petrol engine
F	2.5-litre 200Tdi or 300Tdi diesel engine
L	3.5-litre V8 injected petrol engine
M	3.9-litre V8 injected petrol engine
Y	2.0-litre four-cylinder petrol engine
Steering and Gearbox Specification	
3	RHD, automatic
4	LHD, automatic
7	RHD, 5-speed manual
8	LHD, 5-speed manual
Model Year	
G	1990
H	1991
J	1992
K	1993
L	1994
M	1995
T	1996
V	1997
W	1998
Assembly	
A	Assembled at Solihull
F	Shipped as KD for overseas assembly

Table 2

SAL*	Manufacturer code (Land Rover)
J*	Discovery
G*	100-inch wheelbase
Emissions Specification	
N	50-State emissions (ie California)
Y	49-State emissions
Door Specification	
1	Five-door
Engine Specification	
2	3.9 or 4.0-litre V8 petrol engine
Steering and Gearbox Specification	
4	LHD, 4-speed automatic
8	LHD, 5-speed manual
Security Check Digit	
1 digit; either 0-9, or X	
Model Year	
R	1994 (March to summer)
S	1995
T	1996
V	1997
W	1998
Assembly	
A	Assembled at Solihull

*These codes are sequential and will be present on every Discovery.

Later Discoverys also carry a 'visible VIN', mounted to the dashboard and visible through the windscreen. Here it is on a 1993 model.

How to modify

LAND ROVER

DISCOVERY, DEFENDER & RANGE ROVER

for high performance & serious off-road action

Ralph Hosier

Land Rover Discovery 1989 to 1998, Land Rover 90, 110 and Defender
1983 to 2010, Range Rover 1970 to 1995

**Also includes information on servicing, repair, racing,
expeditions and trekking, plus a buyers' guide**

Buying a Range Rover, Land Rover Discovery or Defender can be just the start of a
wonderful adventure. This book describes the options available to the owner, from
big wheels and suspension lifts, under-body protection and tuning ideas, right up to
how to convert the car into a high speed racer or an international expedition vehicle.
With clear, jargon-free instructions, advice on events like family weekend green-
laning, international expeditions and full-on competition, accompanied by colour
photographs throughout, this is the definitive guide to getting the most from these
exciting vehicles.

ISBN: 978-1-845843-15-1
Paperback • 25x20.7cm • 128 pages • 312 colour pictures

For more information and price details, visit our website at www.veloce.co.uk
email: info@veloce.co.uk • Tel: +44(0)1305 260068